MW01196938

1

Essential
Music Theory

Mark Sarnecki

**San Marco
Publications**

ISNB: 9781896499236

Contents

1

Pitch and Notation

Sound - Good Vibrations!

Music is **sound**. Sound is all over the place, and you have two fantastic devices that let you hear it: your ears! Sound is created by a vibrating object, like a string, a drum head, a column of air, or a metal or wooden bar. These vibrations are sent to the ear as sound waves.

The ear is a complicated thing. The external or fleshy outer ear is called the **pinna** or **auricle** and acts like a funnel to bring sounds into your inner ear. The inner ear is called the **cochlea** and is a small curled tube filled with fluid that takes sound vibrations or sound waves and creates signals through nerve impulses that the brain interprets as sound. You turn on the music, the vibrations go into your ears, your brain decodes them, and you hear your favorite song.

Figure 1.1

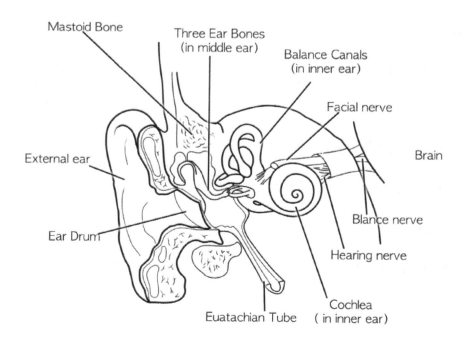

1

Pitch and Intensity

With the ability to hear it is not surprising that humans started to create and organize sounds into patterns that became music.

Sounds can be heard as high or low. This is called **pitch**. The faster an object like a string vibrates, the higher the pitch, the slower it vibrates, the lower the pitch. On a keyboard the higher pitched sounds are on the right and the lower pitched sounds are on the left (Figure 1.2). Understanding the keyboard when studying music theory is helpful.

Figure 1.2

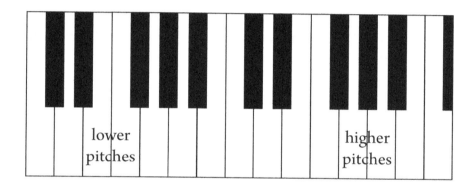

As well as pitch, music occurs in different degrees of loudness or softness. This is called **intensity**. Intensity is determined by how much power is sent to the ear by the sound wave. If you play a really loud chord on the piano with all your strength, a powerful wave is sent to your ear, and the sound intensity is loud.

Pitch may also be defined as the name of the note that you play on your instrument. The system that we use to identify different pitches is achieved by placing notes on a set of lines or spaces called the **staff**.

The Staff

Sound and music have been with us since the beginning of time. Like our languages, it was around a long time before it was written down. Originally it was taught by rote, which means it was learned by listening to it and copying what was played or sung. There was no notation. People just copied the sounds they heard.

Music has been written down for about 1000 years. This isn't very long in terms of world history. Around the year 500 AD we see the first examples of written western music. Monks in the monasteries of the Catholic church developed a system of writing notes called **neumes** (pronounced noomes). Neumes were small markings that were written above the words of a song that indicated the pitch of a note and how long to hold it. Eventually, neumes were placed on a system of lines. The line indicated a specific pitch. If the neume was above the line the pitch was higher, if the neume was below the line, the pitch was lower.

Over the years composers experimented with different ways of writing music, and around the year 1500 they came up with the system we still use today.

Figure 1.3 shows an early manuscript written with neumes.

Figure 1.3

Pitch and Notation

The staff we use today is an outstanding invention. It is the home for music notes and consists of five lines with four spaces between them. The lines and spaces are numbered from the bottom up. As we study theory, we will learn that most things in music are counted from the bottom up (staff lines, notes in a scale, intervals). Figure 1.4 is a diagram of the staff lines and spaces.

Figure 1.4

Line 5	
Line 4	Space 4
Line 3	Space 3
Line 2	Space 2
Line 1	Space 1

The Musical Alphabet

Every note we play has a name. Music uses a system of seven letter names to identify pitches. They are:

A B C D E F G

There are no H's, W's or Z's. After G, the musical alphabet moves back to A. On the keyboard this can be found on the white keys. Figure 1.5 shows the musical alphabet on the keyboard.

The keyboard is a great visual aid when studying music theory. The way it is laid out helps us understand nearly all of the concepts we will study in this book.

Figure 1.5

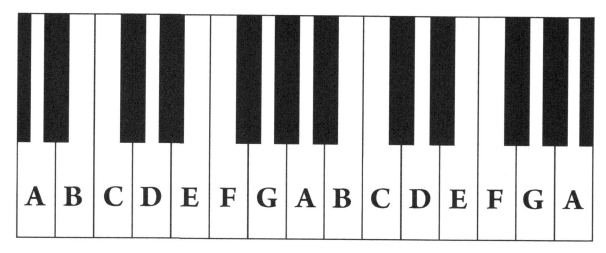

Pitch and Notation

1. Number the lines and spaces on the staff.

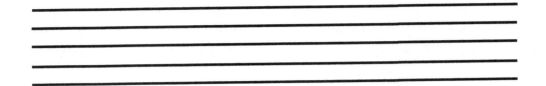

2. Write the musical alphabet on the keyboard.

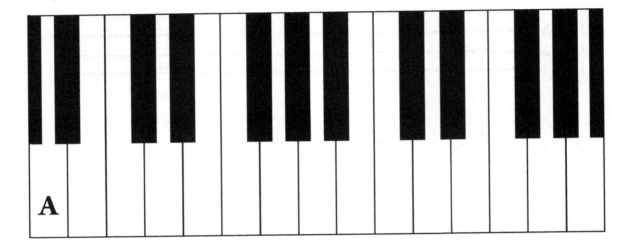

The Treble Staff

We know that the staff consists of five lines and four spaces, but how do we know where the notes are on the staff? To determine this, we need a symbol called a *clef* at the beginning of the staff. The clef defines where notes go on the staff, like a map.

The *treble clef* is the most common clef. It looks a little like a fancy letter G. The inner loop of the treble clef circles around the second line of the staff. The second line is where the note G is located. For this reason, the treble clef is sometimes called the *G clef*.

Figure 1.6

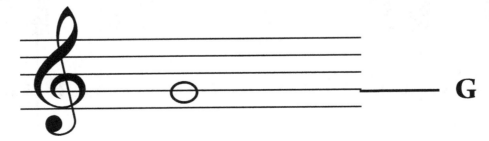

Pitch and Notation

3. Draw several treble clefs in a row.

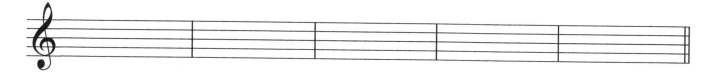

The treble clef is used by instruments with a higher pitch like the flute, guitar, violin, trumpet, clarinet, saxophone and piano.

Space Notes

A space note is a note that occurs within the spaces of the staff. They are placed between the lines without crossing over the lines. When we refer to space notes we say they are **in** a space. For example, in Figure 1.7, the first note is **in** the second space.

Figure 1.7

Line Notes

A line note has a line going through its middle. When drawing a line note be sure that the line goes directly through the middle of the note. Line notes are said to be **on** a line. In Figure 1.8, the first note is **on** line 3.

Figure 1.8

Pitch and Notation

Knowing that G occurs on the second line of the treble staff, using the musical alphabet, it is easy to fill in the remaining notes of the treble staff.

Figure 1.9

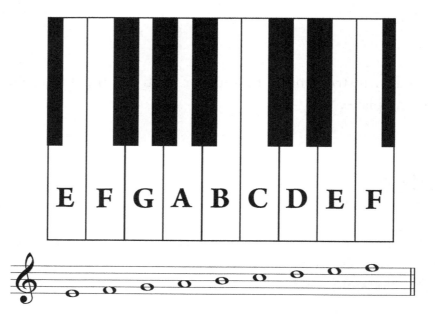

A **mnemonic device** is a great way to help you remember the notes on the treble staff. Mnemonic comes from the Greek word to remember. There are many sayings to help you remember note names.

Figure 1.10 is a saying for the line notes. Can you make up your own? Be careful when you draw a line note. The line must go right through the middle of the note.

Figure 1.10

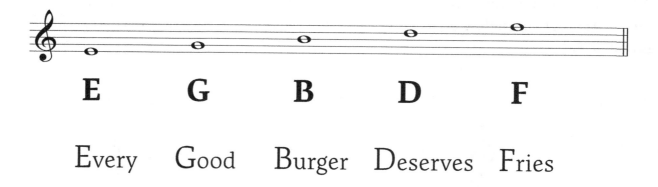

Pitch and Notation

The space notes of the treble clef spell the word FACE. When drawing a space note keep it in the middle of the space and try not to go over the lines.

Figure 1.11

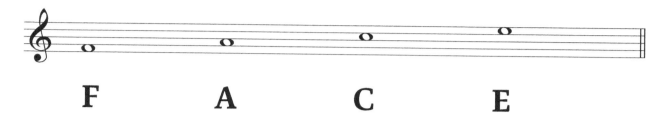

F   A   C   E

1. Name the following notes.

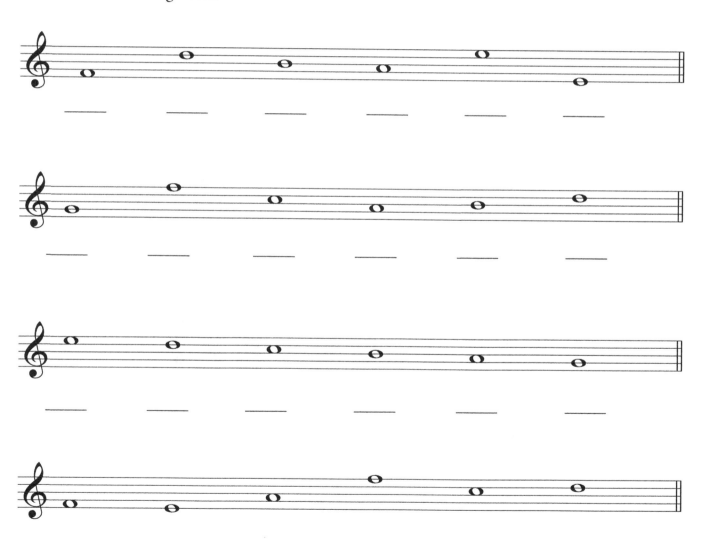

Pitch and Notation

The Bass Staff

The **bass staff** uses the **bass clef** (pronounced: base) and covers the lower sounds in music. The bass clef is sometimes called the F clef because it looks like a fancy F and it has two dots that surround the fourth line which holds the note F.

Figure 1.12

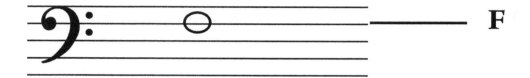

1. Draw several bass clefs in a row.

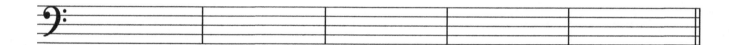

Many lower pitched instruments use the bass clef like the tuba, string bass, cello, trombone, and piano.

Since we know where F is on the bass staff, it is easy to find the other notes.

Figure 1.13

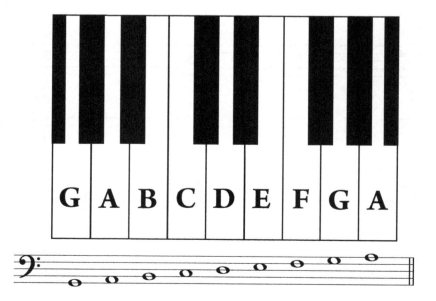

Pitch and Notation

An easy way to remember the notes on the bass staff is to use the sayings in Figure 1.14.

Figure 1.14

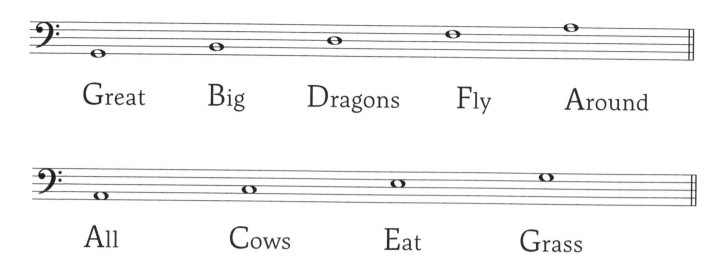

Great   Big   Dragons   Fly   Around

All   Cows   Eat   Grass

1. Name the following notes.

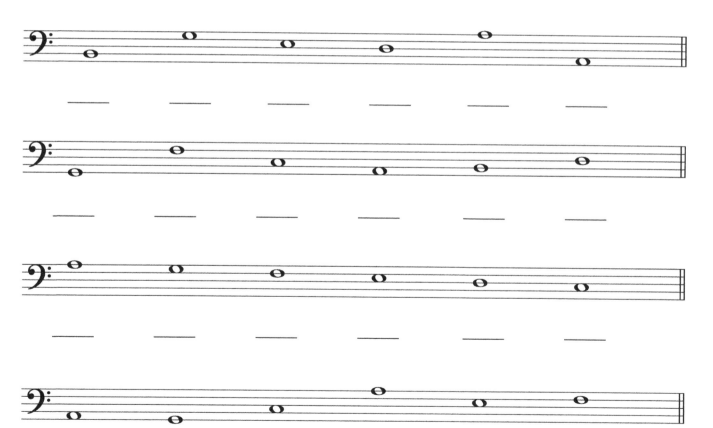

Pitch and Notation

Ledger Lines - Extending the Staff

The staff has five lines and four spaces and holds nine notes. However, there are a lot more than nine notes. The staff can be extended up and down using small lines called **ledger lines**. A ledger line is a short horizontal line spaced the same distance as the lines of the staff itself. It occurs above or below and holds the notes that are higher or lower than the staff. A ledger line is only as long as the note it is attached to, and is never used unless it is attached to a note. The alphabetical order of the musical alphabet continues as you move above or below the staff using ledger lines. At this level, we are going to study notes up to 2 ledger lines above and below the staves.

Figure 1.15 shows how we can extend the range of the staff using ledger lines. The notes move up and down in alphabetical order just like the notes on the staff.

Figure 1.15

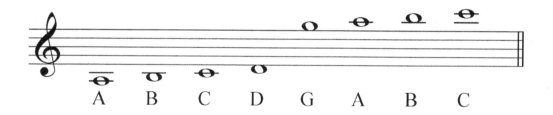

Figure 1.16 shows notes up to 2 ledger lines above and below the bass staff.

Figure 1.16

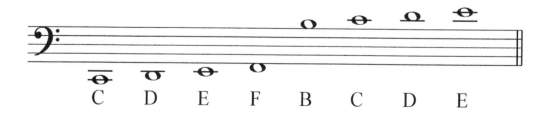

Pitch and Notation

1. Name the following notes.

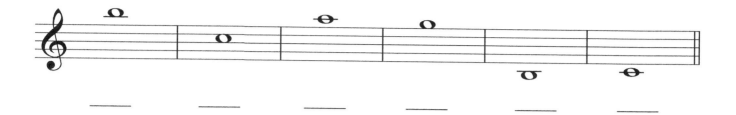

_____ _____ _____ _____ _____ _____

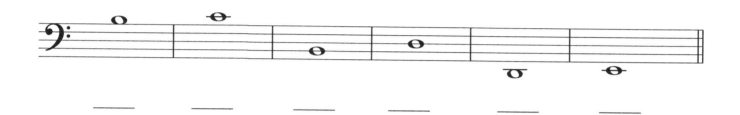

_____ _____ _____ _____ _____ _____

_____ _____ _____ _____ _____ _____

_____ _____ _____ _____ _____ _____

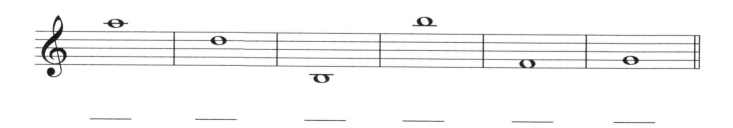

_____ _____ _____ _____ _____ _____

Pitch and Notation

2. Write the following notes using ledger lines below the treble staff.

A   C   B   C   B   A

3. Write the following notes using ledger lines above the treble staff.

A   B   C   A   C   B

4. Write the following notes using ledger lines below the bass staff.

C   D   E   D   C   E

5. Write the following notes using ledger lines above the bass staff.

D   C   E   D   E   C

6. Write the following notes anywhere on the staff.

A   G   E   F   D   C

B   A   G   D   F   E

Pitch and Notation

The Grand Staff

When you combine the treble and bass staves, you get the **grand staff**. This staff is used by the piano because both clefs are needed to cover its extensive range. The treble clef is on the top and the bass clef is on the bottom. They are joined by a line and a brace or bracket. Figure 1.17 contains the grand staff with its notes. Notice that middle C occurs in both clefs in the middle of the grand staff.

Figure 1.17

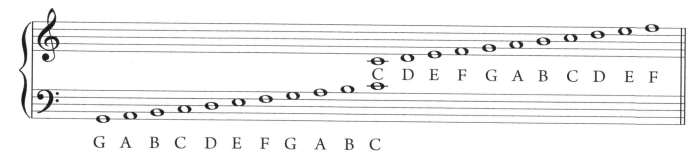

1. Name the following notes on the grand staff.

2. Write the following notes on the grand staff.

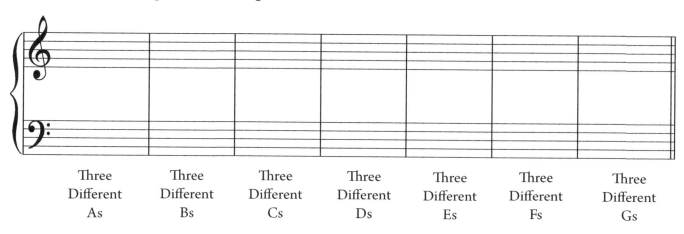

| Three Different As | Three Different Bs | Three Different Cs | Three Different Ds | Three Different Es | Three Different Fs | Three Different Gs |

Pitch and Notation

3. Name the notes and draw lines matching them with the keyboard.

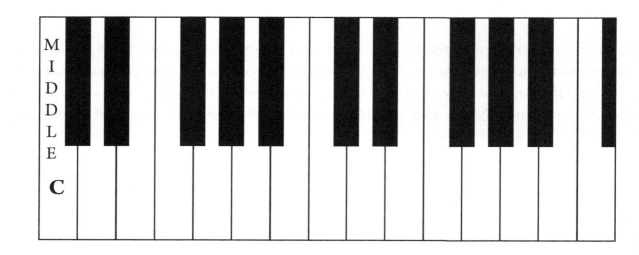

_____   _____   _____   _____   _____   _____

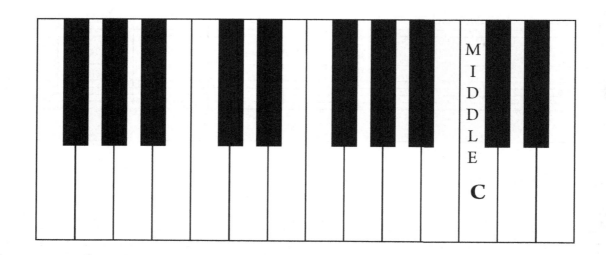

_____   _____   _____   _____   _____   _____

Pitch and Notation

Word Exchange

Name the following space notes which spell words. Write them again in the blank measures using only notes that are on **lines**.

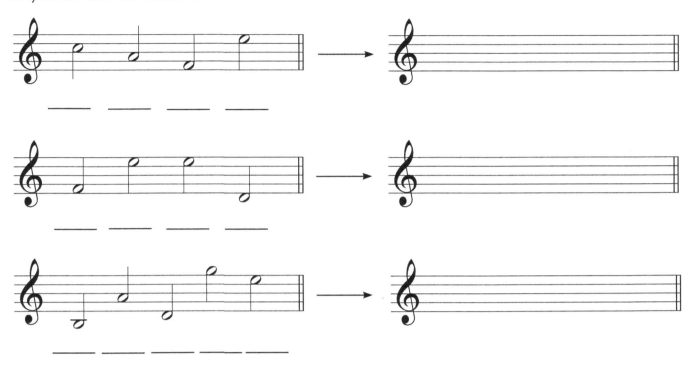

Name the following line notes which spell words. Write them again in the blank measures using only notes that are in **spaces**.

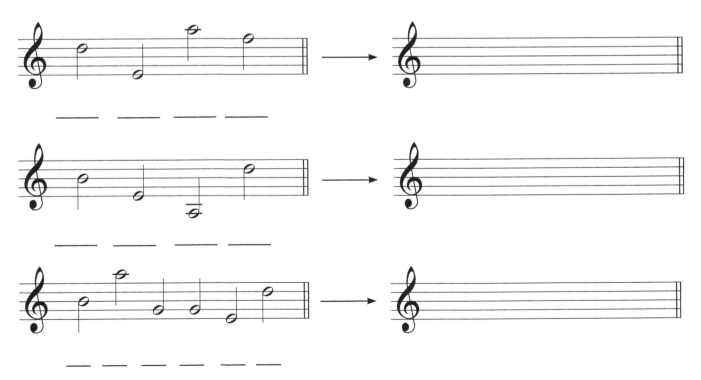

Pitch and Notation

2
Note Values

The Note

Let's talk about notes in general and different types of notes. It is essential to know the various parts of a note and how they work.

The most important part of any note is the **note head**. The note head is the round part of the note. The note head is placed on the staff and gives us the pitch of the note. Note heads are all shaped the same. See Figure 2.1.

Figure 2.1

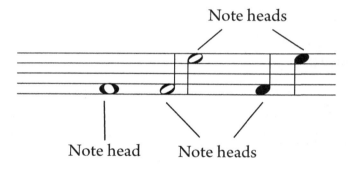

Some notes have stems. The stem is the line that goes up or down from the note head. When a stem goes up, it is placed on the right side of the note head, and when it goes down it is placed on the left side. See Figure 2.2. The length of the note stem is one octave or 8 notes.

Figure 2.2

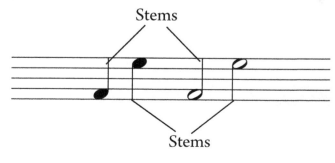

Note Values

In written music, where the note is placed on the staff indicates its pitch, but how the note looks indicates its duration, or how long you hold it. Every note has a value. It might be one beat, or four beats, or two beats. In this level, we are going to learn five different **note values**.

The Whole Note

The note head of the **whole note** is hollow, and it has no stem. This note is easy to detect because it is the only one without a stem. The whole note receives four counts, and its duration is four beats.

Figure 2.3

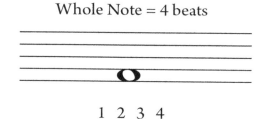

Whole Note = 4 beats

1 2 3 4

The Half Note

The **half note** is a hollow note with a stem attached. It receives two counts, and its duration is two beats.

Figure 2.4

Half Note = 2 beats

1 2

The Dotted Half Note

The **dotted half note** is a half note with a dot beside it. It receives three counts, and its duration is three beats. If the dotted note is in a space, the dot is placed in the same space as the note. If the dotted note is on a line, the dot is placed in the space above the note.

Figure 2.5

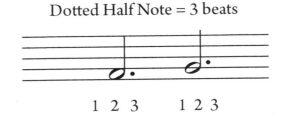

Dotted Half Note = 3 beats

1 2 3   1 2 3

The Quarter Note

The **quarter note** has a solid note head and a stem attached. It receives one count, and its duration is one beat.

Figure 2.6

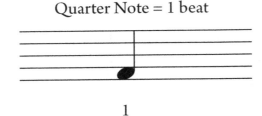

Quarter Note = 1 beat

1

The Eighth Note

The **eighth note** looks similar to a quarter note, but its stem has an attached flag. When two or more eighth notes appear together, the flags are joined by a beam which connects the notes. If we divide the quarter note into two parts, we get eighth notes. Its duration is one half of a beat. Counting eighth notes is a little tougher than the other notes. If you have groupings of two eighth notes, you can count them "one and" with "one" for the first eighth note and "and" for the second eighth note.

Figure 2.7

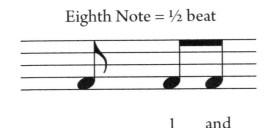

Eighth Note = ½ beat

1   and

Chart of Note Values - It's relative!

Figure 2.8 shows that each note in the chart is twice the value of the one below it.

Figure 2.8

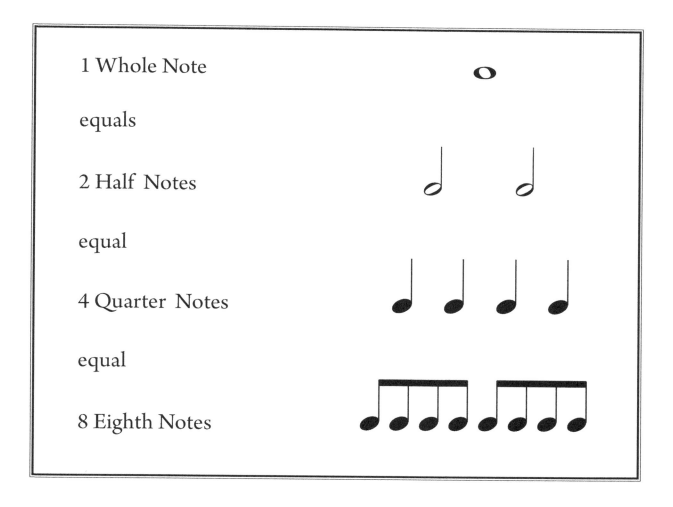

1. Name the type of note or notes.

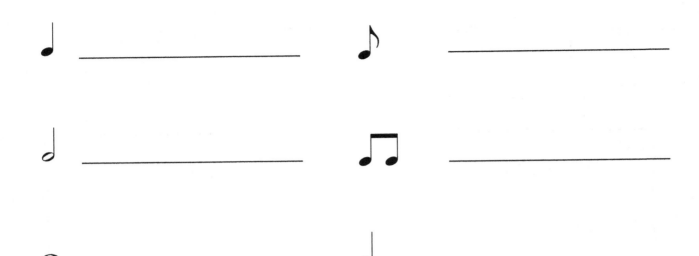

2. Write the number of beats the following notes receive.

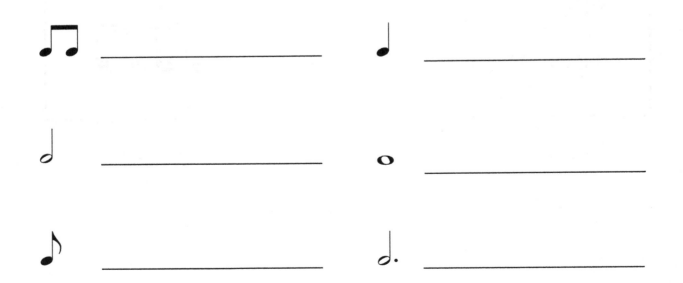

Note Values

3. Write **one** note which is equal to the following groups of notes.

Stems up? Stems down?

A note stem can go up, or a note stem can do down. For a note on the middle line, the stem may go in either direction. It usually depends on the other notes. If their stems are all going down the note on the middle line would go down. If they are going up, the note on the middle line would go up. Majority rules! However, if there is no clear majority, the stem of the note on the middle line can go in any direction you choose.

Figure 2.9 shows notes on the third line with their stems going up and down. *The length of a stem is eight notes, also called an octave.*

Figure 2.9

Note Values

If a note is below the third line, its stem goes up. Be sure to place the stem on the right side of the note when it goes up.

Figure 2.10 shows notes below the third line. The note on the third line has its stem going up. It follows the majority of the other notes whose stems also go up.

Figure 2.10

If a note is above the third line, its stem goes down. Be sure to place the stem on the left side of the note when it goes down.

Figure 2.11 shows notes above the third line. The note on the third line has its stem going down. It follows the direction of the other notes whose stems go down.

Figure 2.11

1. Add stems to the following notes.

3
Rests

Silence is Golden

Mozart said: "Notes are silver, rests are golden." Silence in music is as important as sound. Silence in music is shown with **rests**. The name and length of the rests are the same as the name and length of the notes we studied in the last lesson.

The Whole Rest

A whole rest is four beats long and indicates four counts of silence. The whole rest hangs from the fourth line. It is also used to indicate one whole measure of rest.

Figure 3.1

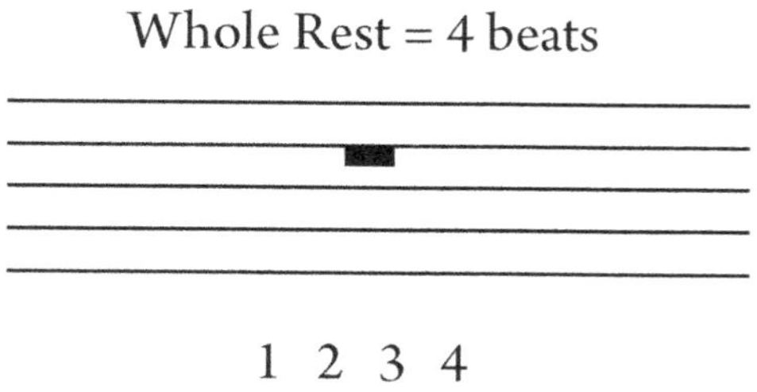

Whole Rest = 4 beats

1 2 3 4

1. Draw a line of whole rests on the staff below.

The Half Rest

A half rest is two beats long and indicates two counts of silence. The half rest sits on the third line.

Figure 3.2

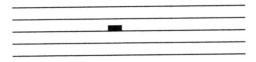

Half Rest = 2 beats

1 2

2. Draw a line of half rests on the staff below.

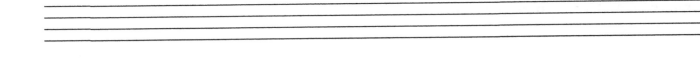

The Quarter Rest

A quarter rest is one beat long and indicates one count of silence. The quarter rest is tricky to draw. Study its shape.

Figure 3.3

Quarter Rest = 1 beats

1

3. Draw a line of quarter rests on the staff below.

Rests

The Eighth Rest

An eighth rest is one half of a beat in duration and indicates one half of a count of silence. The eighth rest is placed in the middle of the staff and looks a little like the number 7.

Figure 3.4

Eighth Rest = ½ beat

4. Draw a line of eighth rests on the staff below.

5. Name the following notes and rests.

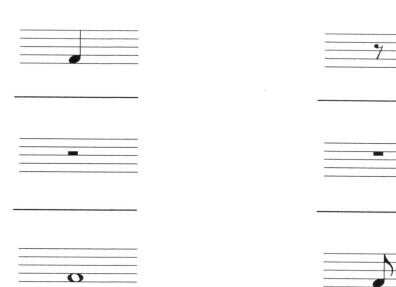

Rests

6. Draw the equivalent rest for each note.

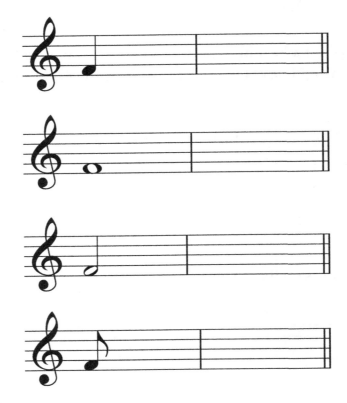

7. Draw **one** rest which is equal to the following notes.

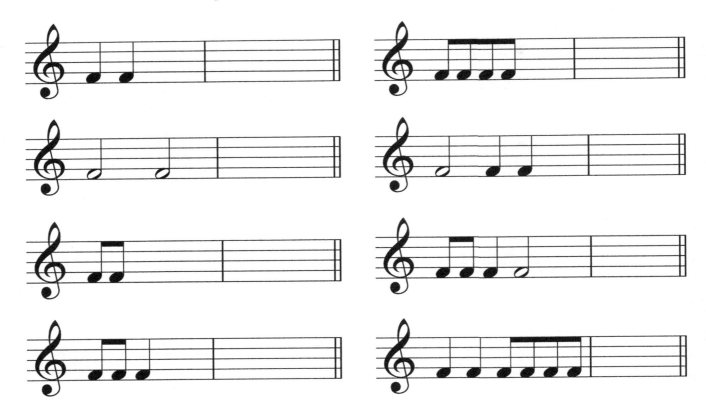

Rests

Music Terms

Music terms are used to tell a performer what to do when playing a piece of music. How loud or soft to play. How fast to play. How long or short to play a note. Most music terms are written in Italian. In the beginning of the 16th century, there was a lot of music being composed in Italy, and composers started to write directions for performing their music. These composers were Italian, so they wrote the instructions in Italian. We also see some music terms in German and French, but the majority are in Italian. It has become a universal language for music terminology.

Dynamics

Dynamics is the word used for how loud or soft we play. The two most important words dealing with dynamics are *piano* (soft) and *forte* (loud). Almost all other dynamics are related to these two words. Study Figure 3.5 which is a chart of dynamic markings.

Figure 3.5

ITALIAN TERM	ABBREVIATION	MEANING
piano	*p*	soft
mezzo piano	*mp*	medium soft
mezzo forte	*mf*	medium loud
forte	*f*	loud

In the 19th century, composers started writing music that had sections that gradually grew louder or became softer. The Italian term for growing louder is **crescendo**. The Italian word for becoming softer is **decrescendo** or **diminuendo**. These terms may be abbreviated as **cresc.**, **decresc.** or **dim.** Figure 3.6 shows the diagrams that represent **crescendo** and **decrescendo**.

Figure 3.6

crescendo   *decrescendo*

Rests

Review 1

1. Write the following notes on the grand staff.

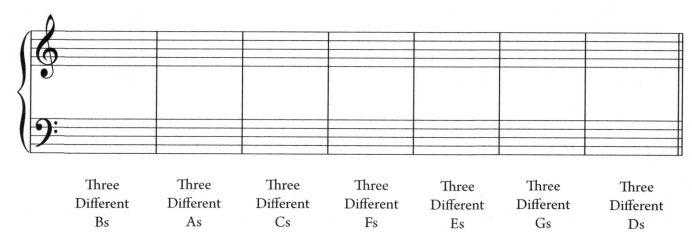

| Three Different Bs | Three Different As | Three Different Cs | Three Different Fs | Three Different Es | Three Different Gs | Three Different Ds |

2. Name the following notes and write the number of beats each receives.

Name: ____   ____ ____   ____ ____ ____   ____ ____   ____

Beats: ____   ____ ____   ____ ____ ____   ____ ____   ____

3. Draw the following rests.

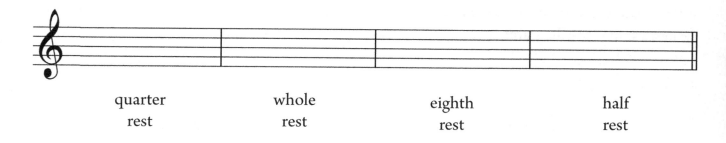

quarter rest   whole rest   eighth rest   half rest

4. Give the name and the meaning for the following musical signs.

Sign	Name	Meaning
p	_____	_____
mp	_____	_____
mf	_____	_____
f	_____	_____

5. Draw the symbols for the following terms.

crescendo _____

decrescendo _____

4
Meter

Bar Lines

The staff is divided into sections by vertical lines called **bar lines**. There are single bar lines and double bar lines. A double bar line indicates the end of a section or the end of a piece of music. You cannot hear a bar line. Its purpose is to make the music easier to read by dividing the music into smaller units or sections.

Figure 4.1

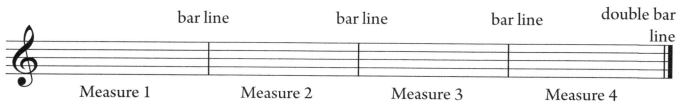

Measures

Bar lines divide the music into sections called **measures**. Figure 4.1 contains four measures. Measures may be different sizes depending upon the amount of beats and notes in the measure.

Time Signatures

Two numbers are placed at the beginning of every piece of music. These numbers are called the **time signature** or **meter**. The time signature tells you how many beats are in each measure. It also shows you which kind of note gets one beat.

Figure 4.2

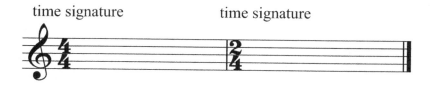

The Top Number

The top number of the time signature indicates how many beats will be in each measure. In the example in Figure 4.3, 4/4 time has four beats in each measure.

Figure 4.3

beats: 1 2 3 4   1 2 3 - 4   1 2 3 - 4   1 2 3 - 4

The Bottom Number

The bottom number of the time signature indicates which note receives one beat. The 4 at the bottom of the time signature in Figure 4.3 means that the quarter note receives one beat. In 4/4 time every measure adds up to four quarter notes. In 2/4 time each measure adds up to two quarter notes. There can be different numbers at the bottom number of a time signature, but 4 is the most common. In this level, we will be studying time signatures which have 4 on the bottom.

4/4 Time

There are many different time signatures. The most common is 4/4. The reason we have different time signatures or meters is that different types of music fall into different patterns. Sometimes words of a song help to shape the patterns in music. A four beat pattern indicates 4/4 time or a two beat pattern indicates 2/4 time. Figure 4.4 is an example where the words to the song help to dictate the time signature. This song has a definite four beats per measure pattern.

Figure 4.4

Fre - re Jac - ques, Fre - re Jac - ques, dor - mez vous? Dor - mez vous?

Common Time

4/4 time is so common you will often see it abbreviated with the letter "C" instead of the numbers 4/4. The C stands for **common** and is shown in Figure 4.5.

Figure 4.5

1   2   3   4

2/4 Time

For the time signature 2/4, there are two beats in each measure and the quarter note receives one beat. Figure 4.6 is an example of 2/4 time where the words to the song help to dictate the time signature. This song has a clear two beats per measure pattern.

Figure 4.6

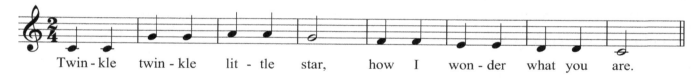

Twin - kle   twin - kle   lit - tle   star,   how   I   won - der   what you   are.

1. Write the beats according to the time signatures under each measure.

Meter

3/4 Time

In 3/4 time, there are three beats in each measure and the quarter note receives one beat. Figure 4.7 is an example of 3/4 time where the words to the song help to dictate the time signature. 3/4 time is sometimes known as waltz time because a waltz requires three beats per measure in order to dance to it.

Figure 4.7

Ear - ly   to   bed   and   ear - ly   to   rise.

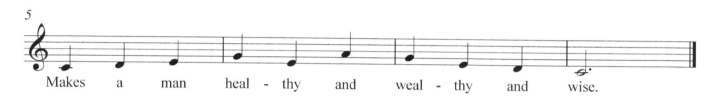

Makes   a   man   heal - thy   and   weal - thy   and   wise.

1. Add **one** note to complete each measure according to the given time signatures.

2. Add time signatures to the following lines.

3. Add bar lines according to the given time signatures.

Meter

4. Add **one note** to complete each measure according to the given time signatures.

5. Add **one rest** to complete each measure according to the given time signatures.

Meter

Tied Notes

A *tie* is a curved line which connects two notes of the same pitch. The time values of tied notes are added together to make a longer note - you only play the note once.

*Be careful not to confuse ties and slurs! A tie looks like a **slur** - but a slur connects two notes of a different pitch and indicates that the notes are to be played smoothly.* Figure 4.8 shows two tied Fs; the second example shows an F slurred to a G.

Figure 4.8

One reason we use a tie is to hold a note across a bar line. In Figure 4.9 the G is held for three beats.

Figure 4.9

Ties are usually written on the opposite side of a musical note to its stem. In Figure 4.10, the Fs are written stems up, so the tie is drawn below the notes. The Es have stems down, so the ties are drawn above the notes.

Figure 4.10

1. Write the counts under each measure. State how many beats each tied note receives. The first one is started for you.

2 beats   ____ beats

1 2 1 2

____ beats   ____ beats

____ beats

____ beats   ____ beats   ____ beats

Meter

5
Accidentals

Whole Steps and Half Steps

In the music we are studying, the smallest distance between two notes is a **half step**. On the keyboard, it is the distance from one key to the next closest key, black or white. This may mean a white key to a black key, a black key to a white key, or sometimes a white key to a white key. There is a half step between the two white keys E and F and B and C. With these notes there is no black key involved.

A **whole step** is twice as big as a half step. A whole step consists of two keys with another key, black or white, between them.

Figure 5.1 shows a few half and whole steps on the keyboard. The reason we use the keyboard as a reference is because all the notes are arranged in a simple, easy to understand way. For example, a half step is two adjacent keys on the keyboard. We will learn that almost all white keys are natural notes and black keys are notes with accidentals.

Figure 5.1

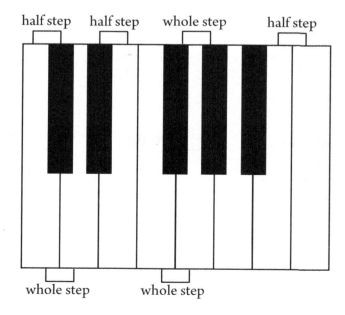

Pitch

The pitch (how high or low it sounds) of a note can be changed. We use symbols placed in front of the note called **accidentals** to raise or lower its pitch.

There are three types of accidentals: **sharps, flats,** and **naturals**. These are shown in Figure 5.2.

Figure 5.2

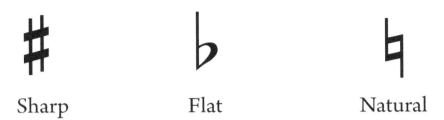

Sharp   Flat   Natural

Accidentals are placed in front of the note that they alter. It is essential to place the accidental before the note, not after it. This can be confusing because when you talk about an accidental you say "*F sharp*", but when you write it on the music score you write it sharp F. See Figure 5.3.

Figure 5.3

F sharp

When you write an accidental it should be written in the same space or on the same line as the note it is altering. Sharps, flats, and naturals have an open space that is placed in the same space or on the same line as the note they are altering.

The Sharp

A **sharp** is an accidental that raises the pitch of a note one half step. It looks like a number symbol. The square in the middle of the sharp should be centered on the same line or space as the note. A sharp sign can go in front of any note. Figure 5.4 contains the sharps located on the black keys of the keyboard.

Figure 5.4

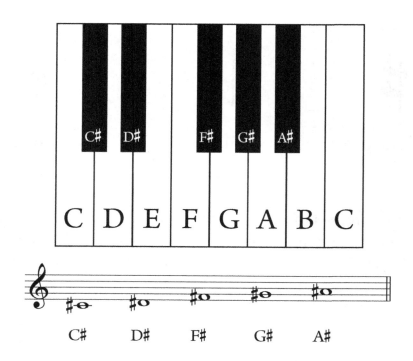

1. Write the following notes. Use whole notes.

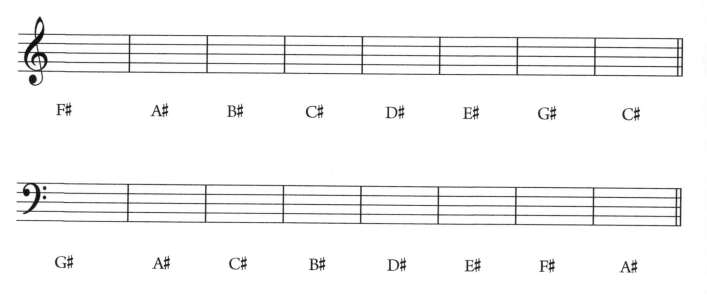

Accidentals

The Flat

A **_flat_** is an accidental that lowers the pitch of a note one half step. Flats look similar to the letter b. The open part of the flat sits directly on the same line or in the same space as the note that it is altering. Flat signs can be used on any note. Figure 5.5 contains the flats located on the black keys of the keyboard.

Figure 5.5

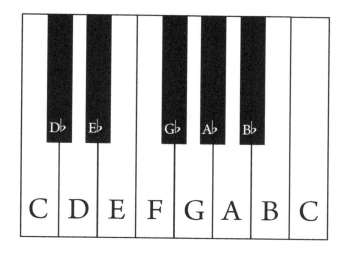

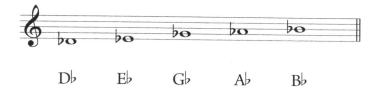

2. Write the following notes. Use whole notes.

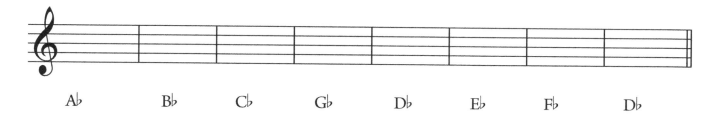

Accidentals

The Natural

A *natural* cancels a flat or sharp. If a note does not have an accidental, it is natural already. When there are not any sharps or flats, the natural is not used. The natural can raise or lower the pitch of a note. If it cancels a flat, it raises a note. If it cancels a sharp, it lowers a note. A natural sign can be used on any note. Figure 5.6 contains naturals on the treble staff.

Figure 5.6

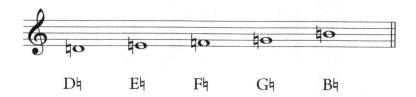

Enharmonic Notes

You can see that each black key can have two names. One sharp name and one flat name. When you have two notes that sound the same or have the same pitch, but different names, they are called *enharmonic notes*. This also applies to some of the white keys. Figure 5.7 contains a keyboard showing enharmonic notes. Notice the enharmonic white keys.

Figure 5.7

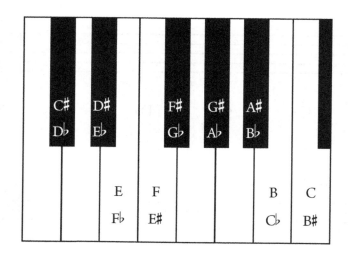

Accidentals

3. Draw lines matching the enharmonic notes.

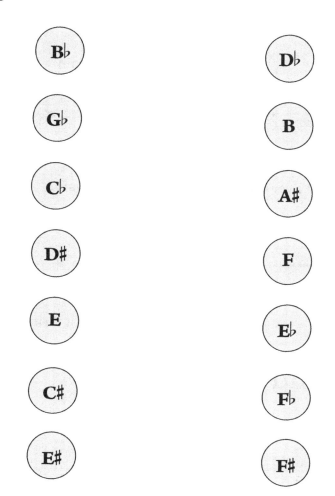

How to Use Accidentals

If an accidental occurs in a measure, it is good for the entire measure. However, a bar line cancels an accidental. In Figure 5.8 the B♭ lasts for the entire measure even though the flat sign is only written once. When the bar line occurs, the B is no longer flat.

Figure 5.8

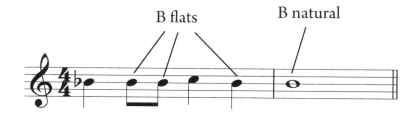

When a note has the same letter name but is at a different pitch, the accidental is written again. In Figure 5.9 the F♯ an octave higher than the first one must be written again.

Figure 5.9

A note with an accidental tied over the bar line is not written again.

Figure 5.10

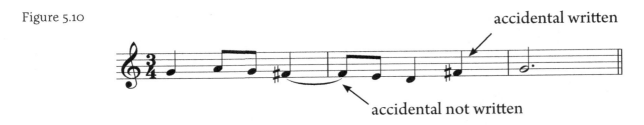

Writing Half and Whole Steps

A half step can be written above or below a note using the same letter name for both notes.

A half step can be written above or below a note using different letter names for the notes.

A whole step is always written using two different letter names in alphabetical order.

Accidentals

1. Name the following notes.

_____

_____

2. Write these notes in both clefs. Use half notes.

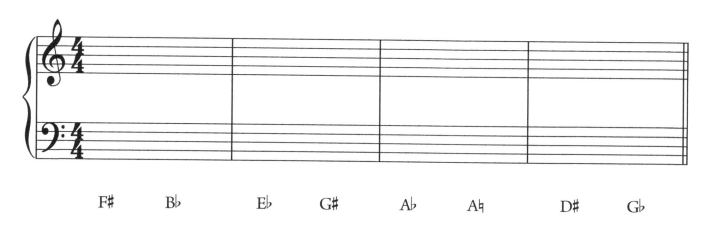

F#   Bb   Eb   G#   Ab   A♮   D#   Gb

3. Write these notes in both clefs. Use quarter notes.

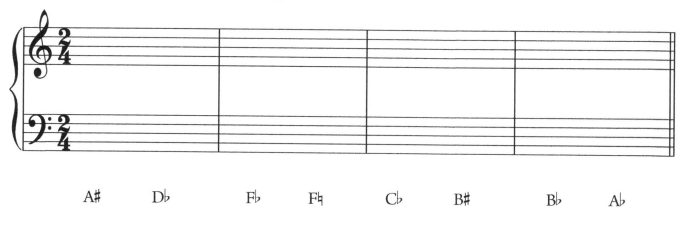

A#   Db   Fb   F♮   Cb   B#   Bb   Ab

Accidentals

4. Name each note and draw a line to the correct key on the keyboard.

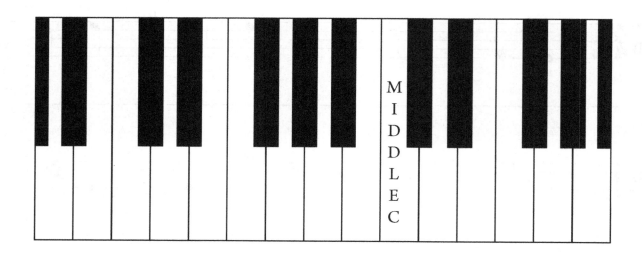

‗ ‗ ‗ ‗ ‗ ‗

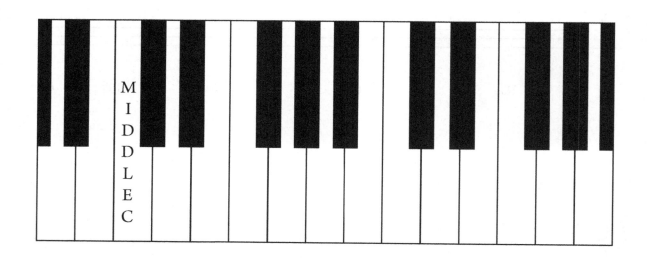

‗ ‗ ‗ ‗ ‗ ‗

Accidentals

5. Describe the distance between the following pairs of notes as a half step or a whole step.

A _____ step   A _____ step   A _____ step   A _____ step

A _____ step   A _____ step   A _____ step   A _____ step

A _____ step   A _____ step   A _____ step   A _____ step

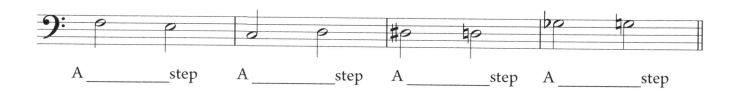

A _____ step   A _____ step   A _____ step   A _____ step

6. Write a note that is a half step above these notes.

Accidentals

7. Write a note that is a half step below the following notes.

8. Write a note that is a whole step below the following notes.

9. Write a note that is a whole step above the following notes.

Accidentals

6

Intervals

Going the Distance

In music, an **interval** is defined as the distance from one note to the next. Intervals are one of the building blocks in music. They are used everywhere, from scales and chords to many more complex musical things.

Intervals are expressed as numbers. For now, we will deal with the intervals from 1 to 8. There are two basic types of intervals: **harmonic** and **melodic**.

- A harmonic interval occurs when two notes are played or sung at the same time.
- A melodic interval occurs when two notes are played or sung one after the other.

Figure 6.1

Harmonic
Interval

Melodic
Interval

Intervals are numbered. To determine the number of an interval, count up from the lowest note to the highest note. This is done even if the lowest note comes after the highest note.

Figure 6.2

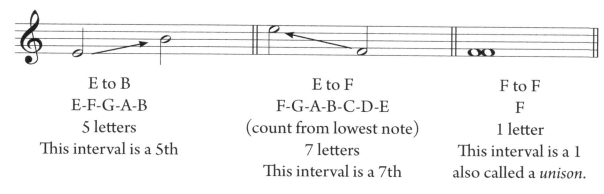

E to B
E-F-G-A-B
5 letters
This interval is a 5th

E to F
F-G-A-B-C-D-E
(count from lowest note)
7 letters
This interval is a 7th

F to F
F
1 letter
This interval is a 1
also called a *unison*.

Intervals

Figure 6.3 contains all the melodic intervals up to an octave. The interval 1 is also called a *unison* and 8 is called an *octave*.

Figure 6.3

1. Write the number name of the following intervals.

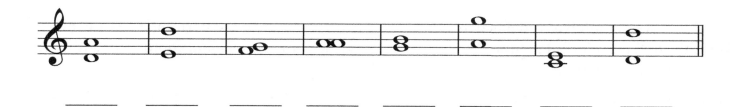

_____ _____ _____ _____ _____ _____ _____ _____

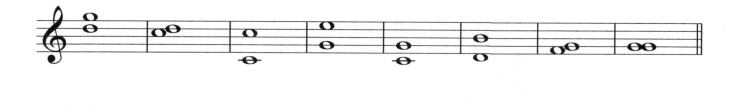

_____ _____ _____ _____ _____ _____ _____ _____

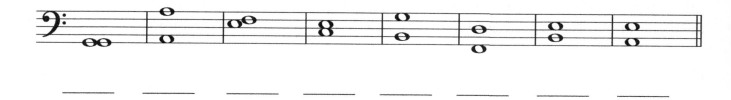

_____ _____ _____ _____ _____ _____ _____ _____

Intervals

2. Write the following harmonic intervals above the given notes.

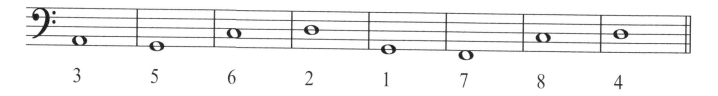

3   5   6   2   1   7   8   4

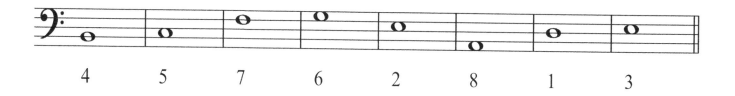

4   5   7   6   2   8   1   3

8   3   4   5   2   1   6   7

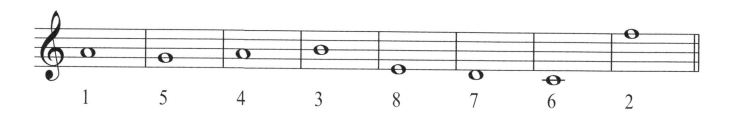

1   5   4   3   8   7   6   2

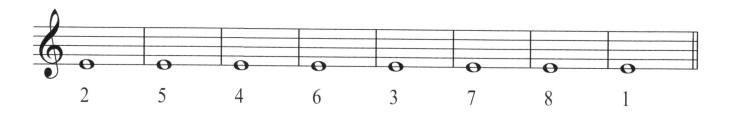

2   5   4   6   3   7   8   1

Intervals

3. Write the following melodic intervals above the given notes.

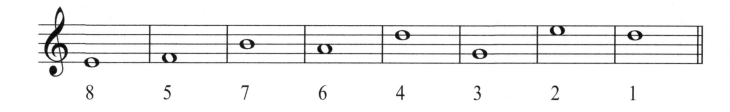

8   5   7   6   4   3   2   1

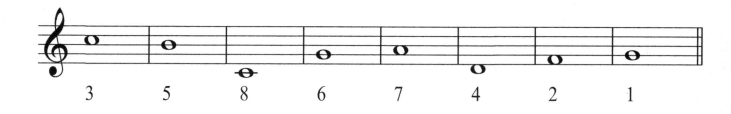

3   5   8   6   7   4   2   1

7   2   3   4   1   8   5   6

8   1   7   2   6   3   5   4

Intervals

7
History 1

Review - The Orchestra

An **orchestra** is a performing group made up of many different musical instruments. Orchestra is a Greek word that originally referred to the area directly in front of a stage. When you attend an orchestral performance, you will see the orchestra playing in that exact place.

The orchestra as we know it today began with Italian opera around the year 1600. Opera was a sung play composed for singers and accompanied by a group of musicians that sat in front of the stage. Early orchestras performed short pieces called **overtures** before the opera started.

The music produced by these groups became so popular that composers started to write large pieces exclusively for them called **symphonies**. This is the reason orchestras are often called 'symphony orchestras.'

By the middle of the 19th century, these orchestras developed a standard group of instruments that has remained to the present day. The modern orchestra contains four main instrument sections:

- **strings** (violin, viola, cello, bass)
- **woodwinds** (flute, clarinet, oboe, bassoon, piccolo, English horn)
- **brass** (trumpet, trombone, tuba, French horn)
- **percussion** (timpani, drums, triangle, gong, cymbals, xylophone, piano, tambourine, +)

To keep the orchestra together, and help them play with the correct rhythm and expression, a **conductor** stands in front of them and directs them using hand gestures.

Camille Saint-Saens (1835 - 1921) Romantic Era

Camille Saint-Saens was born October 9, 1835, in Paris, France. He began studying piano at age two and a half and wrote his first piano piece when he was three. He started performing when he was a young boy and made his Paris recital debut at the age of ten.

Saint-Saens was not just brilliant at music. He also excelled at mathematics and science. He studied music at the Paris Conservatoire and won many prizes there. He became a follower of the great virtuoso pianist, organist, and composer, Franz Liszt.

Saint-Saens composed almost every kind of musical work including symphonies, concertos, and operas. One of his compositions, the Carnival of the Animals, was written as a sort of joke, but it is now his most famous work. He also wrote, books, poetry, and plays.

Saint-Saens influenced other well know French composers, especially Maurice Ravel and Gabriel Fauré.

Saint-Saens is considered a Romantic composer. The Romantic era was a period in time from approximately 1820 to 1910. There are many great composers from this era including:

- Frédéric Chopin
- Robert Schumann
- Felix Mendelssohn
- Johannes Brahms
- Pyotr Tchaikovsky
- Franz Liszt
- Hector Berlioz

The Carnival of the Animals

One of Saint-Saens most well-known compositions is ***The Carnival of the Animals***. It is written for two pianos and orchestra. He had fun describing some of his friends as animals. This piece is known throughout the world for its musical portrayal of animals. Some of the animals he portrays in music include the lion, hens and roosters, the turtle, the elephant, the kangaroo, the cuckoo, and the swan. There are also sections describing an aquarium, an aviary, fossils, people with long ears (donkeys), and a pianist. We will discuss the pieces titled: *Kangaroos, Aquarium,* and *The Swan.* The Carnival of the Animals is *descriptive* or **program music**. Program music is designed to portray a picture, object or story with sound.

Kangaroos

Saint-Saens wrote *Kangaroos* for two pianos. The main melody features hopping 5ths in the theme. When they go up, the tempo gradually speeds up, and the dynamics get louder. When the fifths go down, the tempo gradually slows down, and the dynamics get quieter.

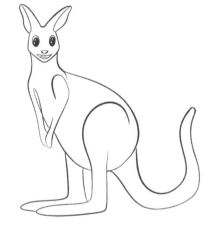

Aquarium

Aquarium is written for two pianos, strings, flute and glass harmonica. In this piece, the composer describes water by trickling runs on the two pianos. The swimming of the fish is portrayed by a smooth melody in the strings and flute. The sound of water droplets was written for the **glass harmonica**, an instrument from the 19th century. It produces a sound much like when you run your fingers around the top of a water glass. It is usually played on the glockenspiel today because glass harmonicas are difficult to find.

The Swan

The Swan is the most famous section of The Carnival of the Animals. It is written for two pianos and cello. A beautiful melody is played by the cello while the pianos play rippling notes and broken chords that describe the swans feet gliding under the water.

Search the internet and listen to a performance of Carnival of the Animals.

Music Signs

Name	Symbol	Meaning
Staccato		play the note short and detached
Accent		a stressed note
Tie		hold for the combined value of the tied notes
Slur		play the notes smoothly connected

1. Define the following musical terms and signs.

piano　　　　　　　_____

forte　　　　　　　_____

crescendo　　　　　_____

mezzo forte　　　　_____

descrescendo　　　 _____

tie　　　　　　　　_____

accent　　　　　　 _____

slur　　　　　　　 _____

mezzo piano　　　　_____

staccato　　　　　 _____

diminuendo　　　　 _____

Camille Saint Saens Crossword

Complete the crossword below.

Word List

Swan
Two
Turtle
Romantic
Elephant
Orchestra
Kangaroo
France
Cello
Donkey
Hens
Glass Harmonica
Two Pianos

Across

3. Chickens
4. Long eared animal
6. Where Saint Saens was born
7. Carnival of the Animals is written for 2 pianos and _____
12. Era in which Saint Saens composed
13. Number of pianos in Carnival of the Animals

Down

1. The Swan is written for _____
2. Rare instrument used in Aquarium
5. Jumping Australian animal
8. Large African animal with trunk
9. Instruments featured in Kangaroos
10. Slow moving animal with shell
11. Gliding water bird

Review 2

1. Add a time signature at the beginning of each line.

2. Add bar lines according to the time signatures.

3. Add **one** rest to complete each measure.

4. Write the following notes. Use quarter notes.

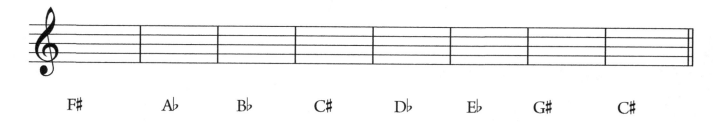

F#   Ab   Bb   C#   Db   Eb   G#   C#

5. Write the following notes. Use half notes.

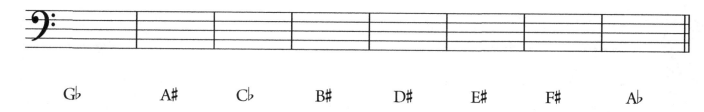

Gb   A#   Cb   B#   D#   E#   F#   Ab

6. Write the number name of the following intervals.

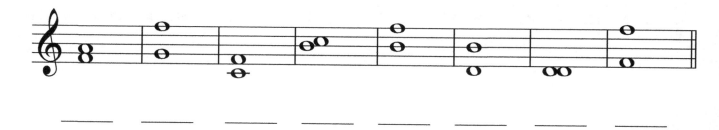

7. Write the following melodic intervals.

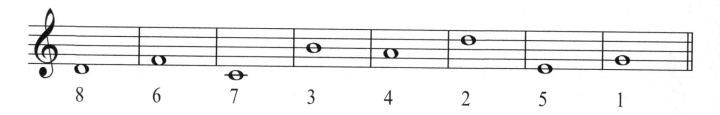

8   6   7   3   4   2   5   1

Review 2

8. Choose the correct answer.

a. An orchestra is led by the:	❏	Pitcher	❏	Conductor
	❏	President	❏	Mayor

b. This instrument is not part of the string section	❏	Violin	❏	Cello
	❏	Viola	❏	Maracas

c. This instrument is not part of the woodwind section:	❏	Flute	❏	Oboe
	❏	Clarinet	❏	French Horn

d. Camille Saint-Saens was born in:	❏	Canada	❏	France
	❏	China	❏	Russia

e. Saint-Saens wrote his first piano piece when he was:	❏	3	❏	2
	❏	10	❏	32

f. Carnival of the Animals is written for orchestra and:	❏	Flute	❏	2 pianos
	❏	3 banjos	❏	Trumpet

g. This animal is not in Carnival of the Animals:	❏	Kangaroo	❏	Elephant
	❏	Wolf	❏	Lion

h. Aquarium is written for 2 pianos, strings, flute, and:	❏	Cello	❏	Horn
	❏	Guitar	❏	Glass Harmonica

i. The Swan is written for 2 pianos and:	❏	Flute	❏	Cello
	❏	Lute	❏	Harp

j. Carnival of the Animals is:	❏	Rock Music	❏	Program Music
	❏	Jazz Music	❏	Opera

Review 2

8

Major Scales

What is a scale?

Almost all music is based on a scale of some sort. Classical, country, rock, pop, hip-hop, jazz, and others are usually built in some way on some scale. The ***major scale*** is the most common scale.

A scale is a group of notes that occur in a specific order. The major scale is a series of eight notes (seven different pitches) that begin and end on the same note. The starting and ending note is called the ***tonic***. The major scale is named after the tonic. If the tonic is C, it is the C major scale. If the tonic is G, it's the G major scale. Figure 8.1 is the C major scale. It starts and ends on C and moves up every note in order. On the keyboard, it consists of all the white keys from C to C. It has seven different notes, C-D-E-F-G-A-B. The eighth note (C) is not counted as a new pitch because it is a repetition of the first note, but the major scale has eight notes in total. Each of these eight notes can be identified with a number with a small tent on top. This tent is called a caret ($\hat{1}$). When a number has a caret on top, it refers to ***scale degree***, which is just the number of the note as it occurs in the order of the scale. The first note is scale degree $\hat{1}$, the second is scale degree $\hat{2}$, etc.

Figure 8.1

Notice that the scale in Figure 8.1 goes from C to C, a distance of eight notes. This is the interval of an ***octave***. From one letter name to the next same letter name, up or down, is an octave. This scale is the C major scale, one octave, ascending.

Building the Major Scale

The major scale is constructed from a specific pattern of whole steps and half steps. All major scales follow the same pattern. Remember that a half step is the smallest distance between two notes. On the piano, it is the distance from any key to the next closest key.

If we examine the C major scale again (Figure 8.2) we can see a pattern of whole and half steps that happens in all major scales. Under the scale you can see whole, whole, half, whole, whole, whole, half. This is the same order for all major scales (WWHWWWH).

The scale can also be divided into two four note sections called tetrachords. Each tetrachord is WWH with a W between the two (WWH W WWH).

Figure 8.2

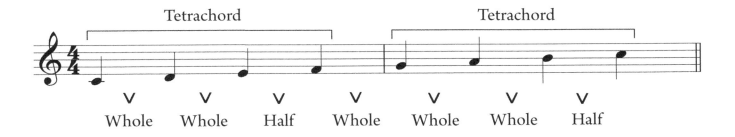

1. Mark the whole steps (W) and half steps (H) under the following scales. Above each one, label each scale degree with a number and caret. Mark the tonic note with a T.

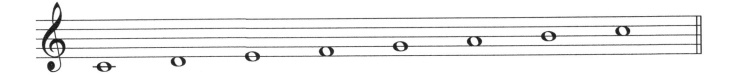

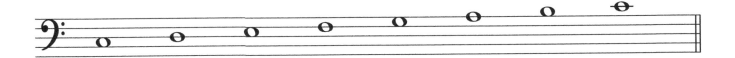

Scale degree one ($\hat{1}$) is called the tonic. This is the most important note of any scale. The second most important note is scale degree five ($\hat{5}$). This note is called the **dominant**. Major scales are most often written and played ascending and descending as in Figure 8.3. Here, the tonic and dominant notes are labeled with T and D.

Figure 8.3

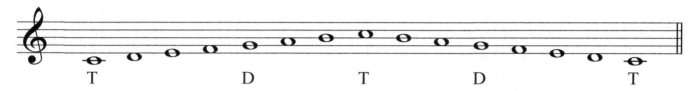

2. Write the C major scale ascending and descending using half notes. Mark the tonic (T) and dominant (D) notes.

3. Write the C major scale ascending and descending using quarter notes. Mark the tonic (T) and dominant (D) notes.

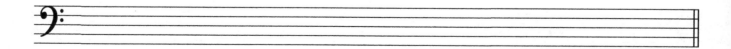

Major Scales

The G Major Scale

Using the same pattern of whole and half steps we can write major scales starting on any note. If we write a major scale starting on G, we must alter one note to get the correct pattern of whole and half steps (WWHWWWH). Figure 8.4 shows that an F♯ is necessary to get the correct pattern of whole and half steps. We need an F♯ between $\hat{7}$ and $\hat{8}$ to have a half step, which also gives us the whole step we need between $\hat{6}$ and $\hat{7}$. The G major scale contains one sharp, F♯.

Figure 8.4

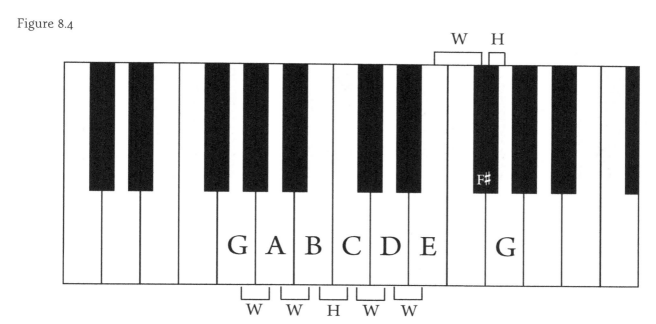

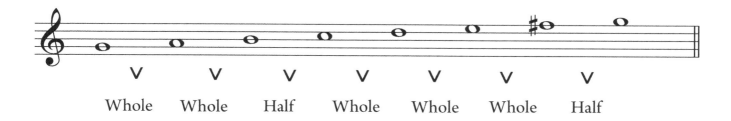

4. Write the G major scale ascending and descending using whole notes. Mark the tonic (T) and dominant (D) notes.

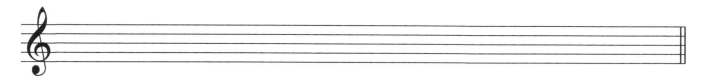

Major Scales

The F Major Scale

For the F major scale, a B♭ is required to have a half step between $\hat{3}$ and $\hat{4}$. The B♭ also creates the required whole step between $\hat{4}$ and $\hat{5}$. E to F is a natural half step between $\hat{7}$ and $\hat{8}$ so they do not need to be altered. This is shown in Figure 8.5. The F major scale has one flat, B♭.

Figure 8.5

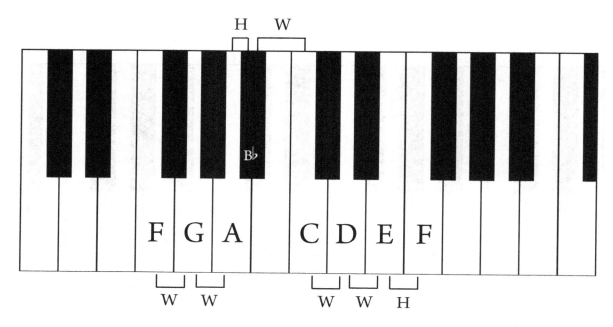

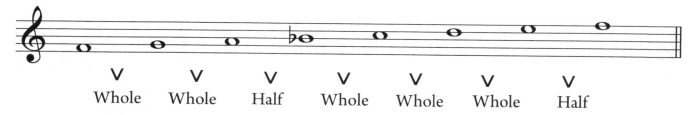

5. Write the F major scale ascending and descending using whole notes. Mark the tonic (T) and dominant (D) notes.

6. Write the following scales ascending and descending according to the instructions.

C major in whole notes

F major in quarter notes

G major in whole notes

C major in half notes

F major in whole notes

Major Scales

7. The following notes are all from the scale of C major. Label each with a scale degree number (1̂, 2̂, 3̂, etc) above each note. Label the tonic (T) and dominant (D) notes.

8. The following notes are all from the scale of F major. Label each with a scale degree number (1̂, 2̂, 3̂, etc) above each note. Label the tonic (T) and dominant (D) notes.

9. The following notes are all from the scale of G major. Label each with a scale degree number (1̂, 2̂, 3̂, etc) above each note. Label the tonic (T) and dominant (D) notes.

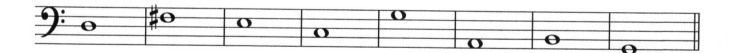

Major Scales

9
Key Signatures

What is a key signature?

The *key signature* is an essential element in the organization of music. Instead of writing all the accidentals throughout a piece of music, composers place them all at the beginning of the staff. The key signature contains the sharps and flats that occur in a piece of music. It tells us the scale the music is based on, and usually the starting and ending notes. It gives us the flats or sharps in a composition. Key signatures never contain both sharps and flats. They will contain all sharps or all flats or nothing at all.

When writing scales in the last lesson, we raised or lowered certain notes with accidentals to get the correct pattern of whole and half steps. Every key signature has the same name as the scale. The key of G major will have the same accidentals as the G major scale (F♯). The key of F major will have the same accidentals as the F major scale (B♭).

The key signature at the beginning of a piece applies to the entire composition unless the composer changes it or adds accidentals. Figure 9.1 shows the F major scale first with accidentals, and then with a key signature. The key signature of F major is one flat (B♭). When it is placed at the beginning of the music there is no need to add B♭'s to the music. The key signature makes all the Bs flat automatically.

Figure 9.1

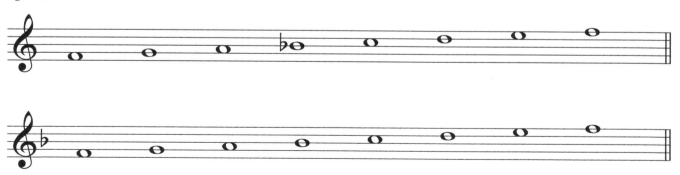

Key Signatures

The accidentals for a key signature are always placed in the same place on the staff. Figure 9.2 shows where they are put on each staff.

In G major the F♯ is placed on the fifth line in the treble staff and on the fourth line in the bass staff.

In F major the B♭ is placed on the third line in the treble staff and on the second line in the bass staff.

Figure 9.2

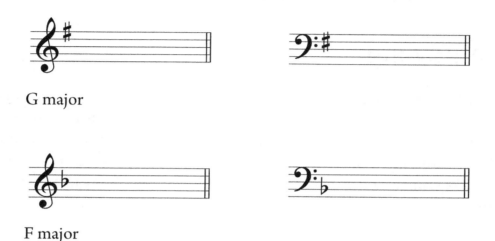

G major

F major

1. Write the following scales in whole notes ascending and descending using a key signature.

F major

G major

G major

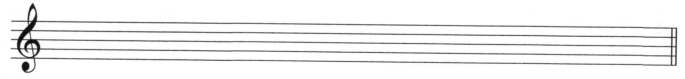

F major

Key Signatures

Key Signatures on the Grand Staff

Figure 9.3 contains the key signatures of F major and G major on the grand staff. The accidentals are always put in the same place in the key signature on the grand staff. Notice that the key signature comes between the clef and the time signature.

Figure 9.3

C major   F major   G major

1. Write the following scales in each clef of the grand staff using key signatures.

F major in half notes

G major in quarter notes

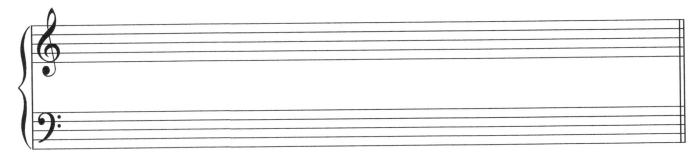

Key Signatures

A key signature identifies a piece of music's 'home base.' The music we are studying is called **tonal music**. In tonal music, the first note of the scale, the tonic, is the most important and central tone. When a piece of music is based on the F major scale, it has a key signature of one flat (B♭) and is said to be *in the key of F major*. F is the most important note, and often (but not always) the piece will begin and end on F. Starting and ending on F establishes the 'home base.'

The melody in Figure 9.4 is in the key of G major. It uses the key signature of G major (F♯) and begins and ends on G, the tonic of G major.

Figure 9.4

G major

1. Name the keys of the following melodies.

Key:_____

Key:_____

Key:_____

Key:_____

Key Signatures

10

History 2

Sergei Prokofiev (1891 - 1953) Modern Era

Russian composer and pianist **Sergei Prokofiev** was born in 1891 in a small village in Ukraine. From a young age, he had a gift for music. Prokofiev began studying piano with his mother when he was three. At five, he wrote his first composition, and at nine, he wrote his first opera. He studied music at the St Petersburg Conservatory from 1904 to 1914.

Prokofiev was a gifted pianist and often performed his works in concert.

Prokofiev's music was more innovative and different sounding than anything ever heard before. It used unusual harmonies and intense rhythms.

After the Russian revolution, Prokofiev moved to America. However, American audiences did not fully appreciate his music. In 1923 he settled in Paris where he was very successful, and his music was well received. In 1936 Prokofiev returned to Russia, where he spent the last 19 years of his life. During this period, he wrote some of his best works.

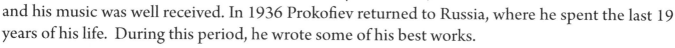

Prokofiev loved to use music to tell a story. One of his most famous compositions that tells a story is **Peter and the Wolf,** which he composed for Russia's Central Children's Theatre. In addition to symphonies, Prokofiev wrote ballets, operas, concertos, piano pieces, movie scores and more.

Peter and the Wolf

Prokofiev wrote Peter and the Wolf in 1936 for narrator and orchestra. It is a story in music that includes both people and animals.

Like Saint-Saens Carnival of the Animals, this is program music. Here, along with a narrator, the music tells a story.

Each character in the story has a particular instrument and a musical theme:

Peter: string instruments (including violin, viola, cello, and bass)
Bird: flute
Cat: clarinet
Duck: oboe
Grandfather: bassoon
Hunters: woodwind theme, with gunshots on timpani and bass drum
Wolf: French horns

Peter, a young boy, lives with his grandfather near a forest. One day, Peter goes out, leaving the garden gate open, and the duck that lives in the yard gets out and goes swimming in a nearby pond. The duck starts arguing with a little bird. Peter's pet cat sneaks up on them quietly, and the bird flies to safety in a tall tree while the duck swims to the middle of the pond.

Peter's grandfather is angry at him for being in the forest alone. What if a wolf was in the forest? Peter says: "Boys like me are not afraid of wolves." His grandfather takes him back into the house. Afterword, "a big, grey wolf" does come out of the forest. The cat climbs into a tree, but the duck, who has jumped out of the pond, is caught and swallowed by the wolf.

Peter grabs a rope and scampers over the garden wall into the tree. He tells the bird to fly around the wolf's head and distract it. Then he catches the wolf by the tail.

Hunters come out of the forest and want to shoot the wolf, but Peter convinces them to take the wolf to a zoo. The narrator completes the story by saying: "If you listen very carefully, you'll hear the duck quacking inside the wolf's belly because the wolf in his hurry had swallowed her alive."

Search the internet and listen to a performance of Peter and the Wolf.

Music Terms

Terms Relating to Tempo

The word **tempo** comes from the Latin **tempus** which means time. Words that deal with tempo are related to how fast or slow we play music. Study the following Italian terms.

tempo	speed at which music is performed
lento	slow
andante	moderately slow; at a walking pace
moderato	at a moderate tempo
allegro	fast
ritardando, rit	slowing down gradually

Sergei Prokofiev
Word Search

```
S T R I N G S D Q O
R E F I V E V C D R
P R O G R A M L U C
J U T Y U I O P C H
H S X C W O L F K E
G S A M O D E R N S
F I B A S S O O N T
D A G O A D C N M R
B I R D G H A E R A
O B O E A T T B E D
```

Word List

Russia
wolf
oboe
five
duck
bassoon
Modern
program
cat
orchestra
bird
strings

1. Where was Prokofiev born? _____

2. At what age did Prokofiev begin composing? _____

3. In what musical era did he compose? _____

4. Peter and the Wolf is written for narrator and _____

5. What type of music is Peter and the Wolf? _____

6. Name 4 animals in Peter and the Wolf. _____ _____ _____ _____

7. What instruments are used to portray Peter? _____

8. What instrument is used to portray the grandfather? _____

9. What instument is used to portray the duck? _____

1. Match the following musical terms to their definitions.

_____ *tempo*

_____ *crescendo*

_____ *moderato*

_____ *piano*

_____ *forte*

_____ *andante*

_____ *ritardando*

_____ *mezzo piano*

_____ *allegro*

_____ *diminuendo*

_____ *lento*

_____ *mezzo forte*

a) moderately loud

b) slow

c) soft

d) becoming softer

e) a moderate tempo

f) moderately soft

g) loud

h) fast

i) becoming louder

j) moderately slow; walking pace

k) speed at which music is performed

l) slowing down gradually

History 2

11
Minor Scales

The major scale evokes a particular color or character in sound. The ***minor scale*** has a different color or character than the major scale. Some might say it is a sadder or darker sound, but that's a matter of opinion. The minor scale is the other main scale in music and occurs frequently. There are a few types of minor scales but we are going to study the natural minor scale. Certain major and minor scales are related because they use the same key signature. Figure 11.1 shows that C major and A minor use the same key signature, no sharps or flats.

Figure 11.1

Key Signature of
C major and A minor

Study Figure 11.2. A is six notes above C. The ***relative minor*** key of every major key is found six notes above the tonic of the major key. Counting up six notes starting on C, (C-D-E-F-G-A) takes us to the relative minor (A minor). A minor is the ***relative minor*** of C major. C major is the ***relative major*** of A minor.

Figure 11.2

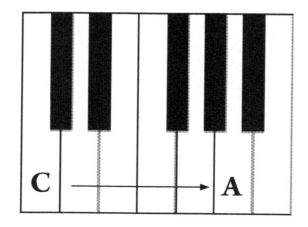

The A Natural Minor Scale

The A natural minor scale is the C major scale played from scale degree $\hat{6}$ (A) to $\hat{6}$ (A). Since C major and A minor share the same key signature, there are no sharps or flats in the A natural minor scale.

Figure 11.3

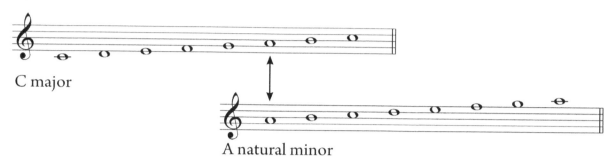

C major

A natural minor

The tonic of A natural minor is A ($\hat{1}$).
The dominant of A natural minor is E ($\hat{5}$).

Figure 11.4

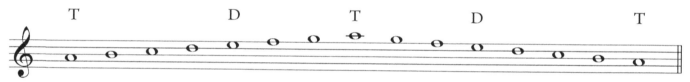

A natural minor scale

1. Write the following scales ascending and descending. Mark the tonic (T) and dominant (D) notes.

A natural minor in half notes

A natural minor in quarter notes

Minor Scales

12
Chords

The Triad

A **chord** is three or more notes sounded at the same time. A **triad** is a three note chord. The **tonic triad** of any key is the triad built on $\hat{1}$ of the scale or the tonic. Figure 12.1 is the tonic triad in C major. The note that the triad is built on is called the **root**. The next note a third above it is called the **third**. The note a fifth above the root is called the **fifth**.

Figure 12.1

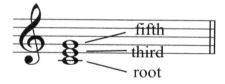

The tonic triad of C major is built on scale degrees $\hat{1}$, $\hat{3}$, and $\hat{5}$ of the C major scale (Figure 12.2). This is also called the **C major triad**. You can build tonic triads in any key by stacking $\hat{1}$, $\hat{3}$, and $\hat{5}$ of the major scale on top of each other.

Figure 12.2

Chords

The tonic triad of G major is G-B-D. It is built like all tonic triads on $\hat{1}$, $\hat{3}$, and $\hat{5}$ of the major scale. The root is G. The 3rd is B, and the 5th is D. This is also called the G major triad.

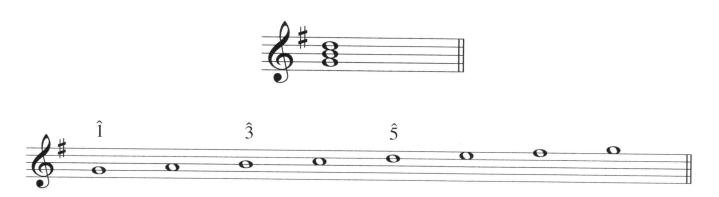

The tonic triad of F major is F-A-C. It is built like all tonic triads on $\hat{1}$, $\hat{3}$, and $\hat{5}$ of the major scale. The root is F. The 3rd is A and the 5th is C. This is also called the F major triad.

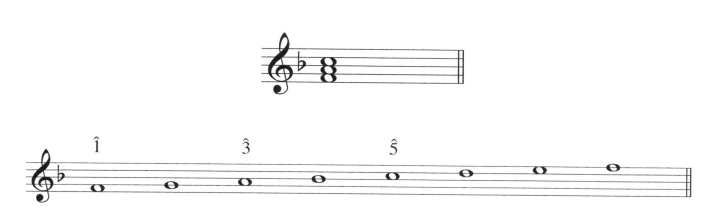

The tonic triad of A minor is A-C-E. It is built like all tonic triads on $\hat{1}$, $\hat{3}$, and $\hat{5}$, but this time we build it on the natural minor scale. The root is A. The 3rd is C and the 5th is E. This is also called the A minor triad.

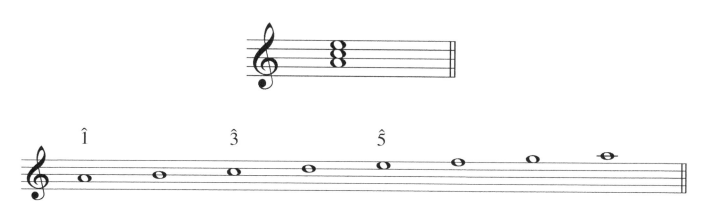

Chords

1. Write tonic triads in C, F, G major, and A minor using key signatures.
   Name the root, 3rd and 5th of each.

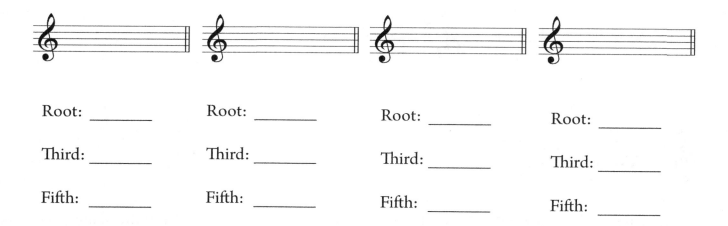

Root: _____   Root: _____   Root: _____   Root: _____

Third: _____   Third: _____   Third: _____   Third: _____

Fifth: _____   Fifth: _____   Fifth: _____   Fifth: _____

Solid and Broken Triads

A triad can be written and played **solid** or **broken**. A triad is solid when all the notes are played together or at the same time as in Figure 12.3. Another word for solid is **blocked**. A triad is broken when the notes are played one after the other as in Figure 12.4.

Figure 12.3   Figure 12.4

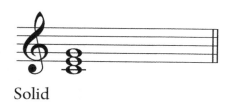

Solid

Broken

Chords

2. Name the following triads as C major, G major, etc.

_____   _____   _____   _____

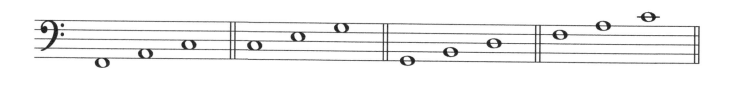

_____   _____   _____   _____

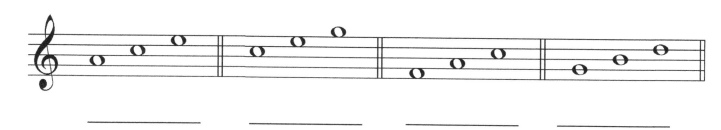

_____   _____   _____   _____

_____   _____   _____   _____

3. Write the following broken tonic triads in each clef. Use a key signature for each.

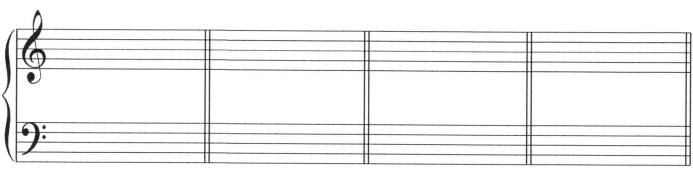

C major   F major   G major   A minor

Chords

4. Write the following solid tonic triads in each clef. Use a key signature for each.

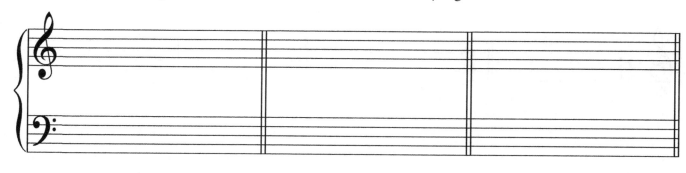

G major   A minor   F major

5. Name the root, 3rd, and 5th of the following triads.

Triad	Root	3rd	5th
F major	_____	_____	_____
G major	_____	_____	_____
C major	_____	_____	_____
A minor	_____	_____	_____

6. Name the key for each of the following. Circle three notes that can form the tonic triad.

Chords

13
Melody

What is melody?

Most musical compositions have a line of notes that are played one after the other to form a tune. This is called a ***melody***. A melody is the main tune of a song. Figure 13.1 is the popular melody 'Mary had a Little Lamb.'

Figure 13.1

The Phrase

Most traditional melodies move in four measure sections called ***phrases***. A phrase is like a musical sentence. Like the sentence in a story, a phrase represents one musical idea. A phrase is indicated by a long curved line called a ***phrase mark***. A phrase mark looks like a large slur. This line indicates the beginning and end of the phrase. Figure 13.1 contains a phrase mark above the melody. This melody is four measures long, which is the most common length of a musical phrase.

How a Melody Moves

The notes of a melody can move in different ways:

- They can move by **step**.
- They can move by **leap**.
- They can move **repitition**.

Most good melodies use all three types of movement. Figure 13.2 shows the three types of movement working together in the first two phrases of the melody 'Twinkle Twinkle Little Star.' Each phrase is four measures long. A leap is the interval of a 3rd or more. Here, the melody leaps a 5th from the last note of m.1 to the first note of m.2. (m. is an abbreviation for the word measure.)

Figure 13.2

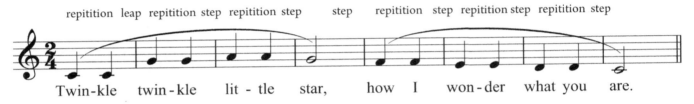

1. Name the key and mark the steps (S), leaps (L), and repitition (R) in the following melodies.

English Folk Song

key:

Norwegian Folk Song

key:

Melody

Writing a Stepwise Melody

In this lesson, we are going to learn to write melodies that move by step. The melody in Figure 13.4 moves by step. It is in G major and uses the notes of the G major scale. It is four measures long and begins and ends on the tonic (G). The tonic is like home base for a piece of music. You can expect to see the tonic used frequently. A piece in the key of G major is all about G. Often a piece in G will start and end on G and contain many G's throughout. G, the tonic, is the star of a piece in G major. This melody has a natural arch that peaks at E. E is the **climax** or high point of the melody. Many melodies will have one high note that is the climax and not repeated. The rhythm of the melody is indicated above the staff.

Figure 13.4

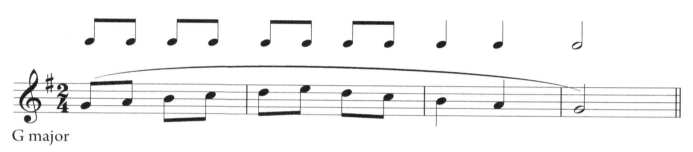

G major

The melody in Figure 13.5 moves entirely by step. It is in F major and uses the notes of the F major scale. There is a compositonal device called a **motive** in this melody. A motive is a melodic and rhythmic idea repeated higher or lower. The motive in m.1 is repeated a step higher in m.2 before the melody steps down to the tonic. This melody begins and ends on the tonic (F). It is the strongest way to begin and end a melody because the tonic is the most prominent note in any key. It clearly establishes F major as the key.

Figure 13.5

F major

Melody

1. Complete this melody using the notes of the C major scale and the given rhythm. Use stepwise motion or repeated notes, ending on the tonic (1̂). Draw a line marking the phrase.

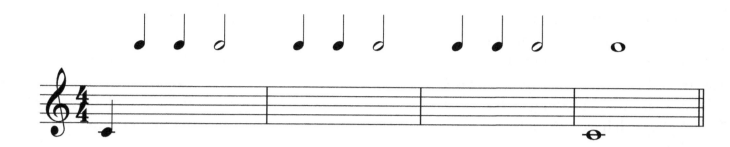

2. Complete this melody using the notes of the F major scale and the given rhythm. Use stepwise motion or repeated notes, ending on the tonic (1̂). Draw a line marking the phrase.

3. Complete this melody using the notes of the G major scale and the given rhythm. Use stepwise motion or repeated notes, ending on the tonic (1̂). Draw a line marking the phrase.

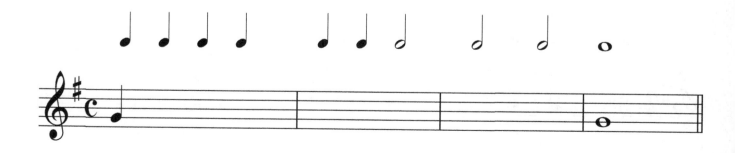

Melody

14

Music Analysis

All of the concepts we have studied in theory can be put to good use when we look at a piece of music. **Music analysis** is studying a composition and figuring out its features. In this lesson, we are going to look at music and answer questions using the information we have learned.

1. Answer the questions relating to the following melodies.

a. Add the correct time signature directly on the music.

b. Name the key of this piece._____

c. Name the interval number at A._____

d. Find and circle a C major triad. Label it "C."

e. Find and circle a G major triad. Label it "G."

f. Define *Moderato*._____

g. Name and define the sign at letter B._____

h. Find a motive and draw a square around each time it occurs.

i. How many slurs are in this piece? _____

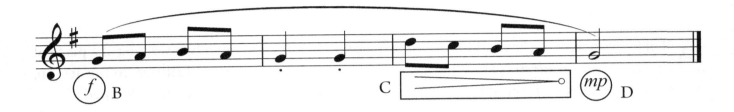

a. Add the correct time signature directly on the music.

b. Name the key of this piece._____

c. Circle each time motive "a" appears in this piece.

d. How many phrases are in this piece? _____.

e. On which scale degree does phrase two end?_____

f. Define **Andante**._____

g. Name and define the sign at letter A._____

h. Name and define the sign at letter B._____

i. Name and define the sign at letter C. _____

j. Name and define the sign at letter D._____

Music Analysis

Bagatelle

Allegro

Anton Diabelli
(1781 - 1858)

a. What is the title of this piece? _____

b. Who is the composer? _____

c. Name the key of this piece._____

d. Add the time signature directly on the music.

e. How many phrases are in this piece? _____.

f. On which scale degree does the melody of this piece begin?_____

g. Define *Allegro*._____

h. Name the interval number at A._____

i. Name the interval number at B._____

j. This piece is played:

       ❑loud   ❑soft

Music Analysis

Review 3

1. Write the following scales ascending and descending using key signatures. Mark the tonic (T) and dominant (D) notes.

G major in quarter notes

F major in half notes

A natural minor in whole notes

2. Write the following tonic triads in broken form using a key signature.

C major   G major   F major   A minor

3. Write the following tonic triads in solid form using a key signature.

F major   G major   C major   A minor

4. Complete this melody using the notes of the G major scale and the given rhythm. Use stepwise motion or repeated notes, ending on the tonic ($\hat{1}$). Draw a slur over the phrase.

5. Draw lines to match the instrument with the character it represents in 'Peter and the Wolf. '

Wolf	Strings
Peter	French Horns
Hunters	Bassoon
Cat	Oboe
Duck	Clarinet
Bird	Timpani
Grandfather	Flute

6. Answer true (T) or false (F) to the following statements.

a. **Common time** is another name for 2/4 time. _____

b. *ritardando* means to become softer. _____

c. *allegro* means fast. _____

d. *tempo* is the speed which music is performed. _____

e. *andante* means to slow down. _____

f. *lento* means slow. _____

g. *decrescendo* and *diminuendo* mean the same thing. _____

7. Give the abbreviations for the following music terms.

a. *ritardando* _____

b. *diminuendo* _____

c. *crescendo* _____

d. *decrescendo* _____

e. *mezzo piano* _____

f. *fortissimo* _____

Music Terms and Signs

Terms

accent	a stressed note
allegro	fast
andante	moderately slow, at a walking pace
a tempo	return to the original tempo
crescendo, cresc.	becoming louder
decrescendo, decresc.	becoming softer
diminuendo, dim.	becoming softer
forte, f	loud
legato	smooth
lento	slow
mezzo forte, mf	moderately loud
mezzo piano, mp	moderately soft
moderato	at a moderate tempo
piano, p	soft
ritardando, rit.	slowing down gradually
staccato	play short and detached
tempo	speed at which music is performed

Terms and Signs

Signs

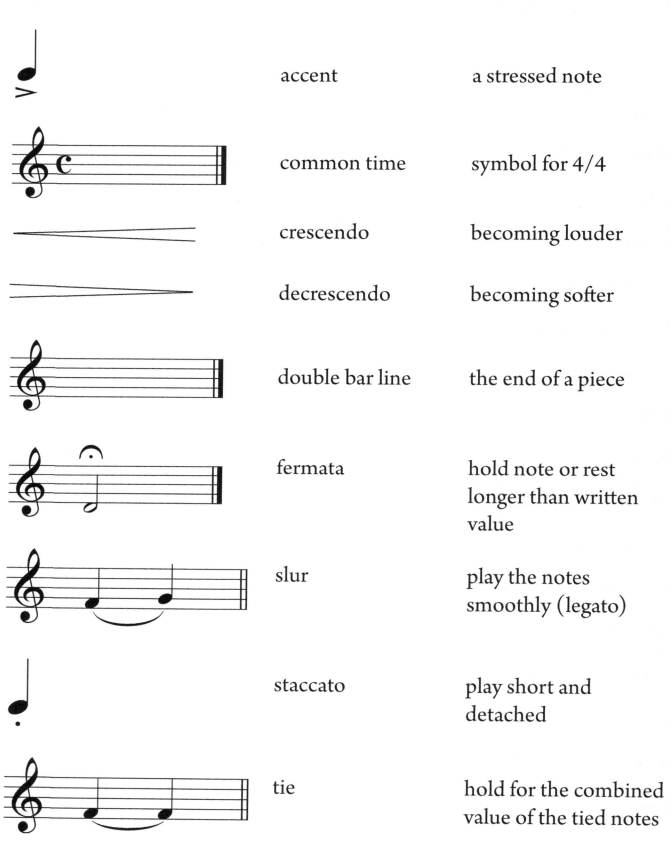

	accent	a stressed note
	common time	symbol for 4/4
	crescendo	becoming louder
	decrescendo	becoming softer
	double bar line	the end of a piece
	fermata	hold note or rest longer than written value
	slur	play the notes smoothly (legato)
	staccato	play short and detached
	tie	hold for the combined value of the tied notes

Terms and Signs

Made in the USA
Middletown, DE
02 October 2023

39981804R00057